FOCUS ON BIRDS

Animal Watch

Stephen Savage

Gareth Stevens
Publishing

Please visit our website, www.garethstevens.com.
For a free color catalogue of all our high-quality books,
call toll free 1-800-542-2595 or fax 1-877-542-2596.

Library in Congress Cataloging-in-Publication Data

Savage, Stephen, 1965-
Focus on birds / Stephen Savage.
  p. cm. — (Animal watch)
Includes index.
ISBN 978-1-4339-5981-3 (library binding)
1. Birds—Juvenile literature. I. Title.
QL676.2.S284 2011
598—dc22

                                   2010049248

This edition first published in 2012 by
Gareth Stevens Publishing
111 East 14th Street, Suite 349
New York, NY 10003

Copyright © 2012 Wayland/Gareth Stevens Publishing

Editorial Director: Kerri O'Donnell
Design Director: Haley Harasymiw

Printed in China
CPSIA compliance information: Batch #WAS11GS: For further information contact Gareth Stevens, New York, New York at 1-800-542-2595.

Contents

What a Difference!   4

Where Birds Live   6

Catching a Meal   8

Hot and Cold   12

Getting Around   16

Hatching and Raising
Chicks   20

Pet Birds   24

Unusual Birds   26

Scale of Birds   28

Glossary   30

Topic Web   30

Activities   30

Finding Out More   31

Index   32

What a Difference!

The main difference between birds and most other animals is that birds can fly.

BIRD CHARACTERISTICS

- Birds are warm-blooded.
- Their bodies are covered in feathers.
- They have two wings.
- They use a bill to obtain food.
- They lay eggs to produce young.

The ostrich is ➡ the world's largest bird. Ostriches cannot fly because they are too heavy, sometimes weighing up to 345 pounds (156 kilograms).

Birds can be very different from each other. Some are large; others are tiny. Many birds have unusual bills. Some have brilliantly colored feathers.

The male bird of paradise has ➡ brightly colored feathers to attract a female.

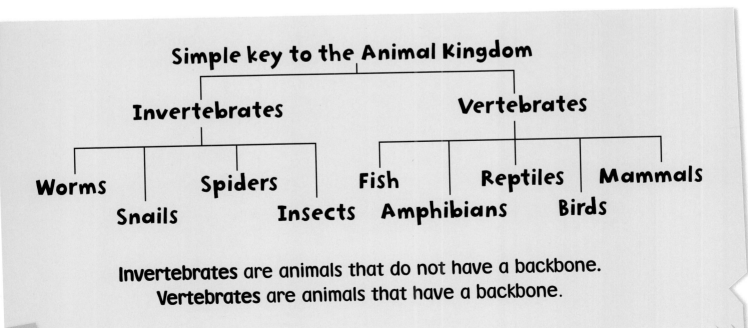

Simple key to the Animal Kingdom

Invertebrates

Vertebrates

Worms

Snails

Spiders

Insects

Fish

Amphibians

Reptiles

Birds

Mammals

Invertebrates are animals that do not have a backbone.
Vertebrates are animals that have a backbone.

Where Birds Live

Birds live in all of the world's habitats, including forests, grasslands, deserts, seashores, mountains, lakes, rivers, and on the sea. Some even live in polar regions.

LIVING IN DIFFERENT HABITATS

- Forest and woodland birds have clawed feet for gripping branches.
- Ducks have webbed feet for swimming.
- Birds that live in water have waterproof feathers.
- Vultures have large wings for gliding over grassland.

← Snowy owls live in the frozen Arctic. Their white feathers keep them warm and camouflaged against the snow.

Birds have special features that help them live in these very different habitats. These features include long legs, webbed and clawed feet, and bills of different shapes.

← The treecreeper has large, clawed feet for gripping bark. Its bill is curved for poking into holes in search of insects.

↑ This stilt has long legs for wading in shallow water and a long bill so it can reach food on the lake bottom.

Catching a Meal

The shape of a bird's bill, or beak, is a clue to the type of food it eats. Eagles have sharp beaks for tearing food into bite-sized pieces.

Parrots and finches use their strong beaks to crack open seeds and nuts or to scoop out fruit. A thin bill is good for catching insects.

↑ The kingfisher dives into the river to catch small fish.

← The pied wagtail eats insects that it catches on the ground or in the air.

↑ A parrot can hold a nut in its foot while breaking the shell with its tough beak.

Hawks and eagles have excellent eyesight to spot small mammals. They dive on their prey, grabbing it with their clawed feet.

← A bald eagle searches the ground, looking for prey.

↓ A peregrine falcon eats other, smaller birds, which it may catch on the ground or in the air.

A few birds use tools to catch food. The woodpecker finch holds a cactus spine in its beak to pull insects from holes in trees. The Egyptian vulture picks up stones with its beak and drops them onto ostrich eggs to break the shells.

Vultures feed on dead animals.

AVOIDING PREDATORS

- Female birds are often brown, so they cannot easily be spotted on their nests.

- The fulmar can spit foul liquid at an attacker.

- Ducks and swans often sleep on water, where they are safe from attack.

Hot and Cold

Birds have soft, fluffy feathers to keep them warm. They must bathe regularly, even in winter, to keep their feathers clean.

Some birds fly to warmer regions in the winter and return the following year. This is called migration.

↑ Many birds have a patch of bare skin on their breast. This mallard uses its body warmth to keep its eggs warm.

← Swallows breed in Europe and North America. In the winter, they migrate south to warmer regions. This swallow is drinking as it flies over a river.

↓ A thick layer of blubber and tightly packed feathers keep emperor penguins warm in the frozen Antarctic.

↑ Arctic terns fly about 22,000 miles (35,000 km) to migrate to warmer climates.

This bee-eater is "gaping" to cool → itself. It may die if it gets too hot.

A bird cannot sweat to lose body heat as most mammals do. It can cool itself by sitting with its bill open, "gaping."

Birds that live in deserts and other very hot regions rest in the shade during the hottest part of the day.

↓ A heron spreads its wings to cast a shadow over the nest to keep the eggs cool.

HOW TO KEEP WARM AND COOL

* Black-necked storks spray their eggs with water to cool them.

* Birds living in cities cool themselves in pools and fountains.

Getting Around

Most birds use their wings to fly. When a bird flaps its wings, the flight feathers in the wings push against the air. This lifts the bird off the ground and pushes it forward.

The wings of a wandering albatross measure 11 feet (3.3 m) from the tip of one to the tip of the other. The albatross can glide for hours without flapping its wings.

A hummingbird hovers by beating its wings 70 times a second. It needs to hover so that it can sip nectar from flowers.

Small birds have short wings that they must flap very quickly. Birds with larger wings flap slowly and can glide to save their energy.

Penguins use their flipperlike wings to swim underwater.

The double-wattled → cassowary cannot fly. It escapes predators by running. It can also swim across rivers.

WAYS OF MOVING

- Birds that fly have lightweight bones.
- A bird uses its tail for steering.
- Emperor penguins toboggan along the snow on their stomachs.
- Mute swans run along the water to take off.
- The flightless ostrich can run at 40 miles (70 km) per hour.
- Swifts spend most of their life in the air, including sleeping in short naps.

There are about 40 types of birds that cannot fly. Many of these have developed large powerful legs for running.

Flightless birds may have lost the ability to fly because they no longer needed to fly to find food or escape from danger.

↓ The roadrunner rarely flies. It uses its wings for balance to run after prey at up to 26 mph (40 km/h).

Hatching and Raising Chicks

Male and female birds come together to breed and raise their young. Some birds sing a courtship song to attract a mate. Others perform a complicated dance.

↓ These Japanese red crowned cranes are performing a courtship dance. They will probably stay together for life.

↑ A female blackbird brings food for her young. The chicks are hatched with few feathers, so they cannot fly.

Most birds lay their eggs in a nest. This may be a simple pile of twigs or a neat, carefully woven nest.

Young swans, called cygnets, follow their → parents soon after hatching. The adult swans teach the cygnets how to survive.

← Plovers nest on the ground. This golden plover pretends it has a broken wing to lure a predator away from its nest.

There are many predators on the lookout for eggs or chicks. Parent birds have to keep a constant watch and will fight off raiders.

↓ Cuckoos lay their eggs in other birds' nests (inset). This little reed warbler is trying to feed the huge cuckoo chick it has raised.

UNUSUAL NESTING PLACES

- Some types of penguins nest in old rabbit burrows.

- The male parent emperor penguin looks after the egg while the female feeds in the sea. He balances the egg on his feet to keep it off the snow.

- European wrens may nest in backyard sheds.

- Mallards sometimes nest in hollow trees.

↓ White storks often build their nests on high rooftops, such as churches.

Some birds nest in large colonies, making it harder for predators to attack. However, squabbles often break out among neighbors.

Pet Birds

TAKING CARE OF PET BIRDS

- Make sure your cage has plenty of space.
- Provide the correct food and water.
- Remember that birds kept on their own need human company.
- Many birds enjoy a spray of fine water.
- Provide a supply of food and water in the yard for wild birds, especially during cold weather.

Birds are often kept as pets, but they need special care. You can study the characteristics of birds by looking closely at pet birds.

Pet parakeets → should be kept in a cage with plenty of space or in an outdoor aviary. In the wild they live in large flocks.

Birds need to fly. When they are young, they can be trained to fly around the room and then return to their cage.

↓ A bird feeder with nuts will attract wild birds, such as these great and blue tits, to visit your backyard.

Cockatoos make good pets. ➡ Like parakeets, they should have plenty of space and company. Pet cockatoos can mimic human words.

Unusual Birds

Many birds have special features that help them survive. For instance, owls have extra large eyes to help them see in the dark.

↓ The secretary bird looks like an eagle on stilts. It kills large prey, such as snakes, by stamping on them.

↑ Pelicans plunge their heads underwater, catching fish in their netlike beaks.

Some birds have unusual habits. Oxpeckers ride on the backs of large grass-eating animals. They feed on the parasites and flies living on the animals' skin, helping to clean the animals at the same time.

UNUSUAL FEATURES

- Pelicans have a beak pouch to store fish.
- A sword-billed hummingbird's bill is as long as its body.
- Hoatzin chicks have claws on their wings for climbing trees in their rain forest home.

Scale of Birds

Human Ostrich Bird of paradise Snowy owl Stilt Bald eagle Peregrine falcon Vulture

Human Roadrunner Swan Japanese red crowned crane Cockatoo Secretary bird Brown pelican Hoatzin Flamingo

Human Fulmar Mallard Emperor penguin Arctic tern Heron Black-necked stork Wandering albatross Double-wattled cassowary

Bee-eater   Hummingbird   Swift   Blackbird   Golden plover   Human hand

Treecreeper   Kingfisher   Pied wagtail   African gray parrot   Swallow   Human hand

Cuckoo   Reed warbler   Parakeet   Oxpecker   Woodpecker Finch   Wren   Human hand

Topic Web

SCIENCE
Classification.
Reproduction—eggs and young.
How birds adapt to their environment—for example, through the shape of beaks and feet.
Food chain.
Predators and prey.

MATH
Compare the sizes of birds with each other and with humans.

GEOGRAPHY
Bird habitats—forests, grasslands, mountains, lakes, coasts, and the polar regions.

ENGLISH
Write a story from the point of view of a bird.

DRAMA/DANCE/MUSIC
Mime how different birds fly and move.
Imitate bird noises.

ARTS & CRAFTS
Make a painting of birds in a habitat.
Make a food chain mobile.

Activities

Science Study the birds that visit your backyard or school grounds to feed. Put out food to attract birds. Try to identify the birds you see using a library book or the Internet. Write notes and sketch the birds that you see.

Drama/Dance/Music Eagles, kestrels, and hummingbirds fly in different ways. Pigeons, woodpeckers, and penguins have different ways of moving. In a group, mime your favorite birds. Can the others guess the birds? You could also imitate bird noises.

Geography Swallows migrate from northern Europe to southern Africa and from Canada to South America. Arctic terns journey from the Arctic to Antarctica. Look at a world map.

Find your country, and compare its size with the journeys of these birds.

Math The chart on pages 28-29 shows the size of birds compared to an adult human. Estimate your size against the human figure. Make a list of all the birds that are taller than you.

Arts & Crafts On a large piece of paper, draw a picture of a habitat, such as a forest, lake, or the seashore. Now draw and color in the birds that live there. A library book or the Internet can help you.

English Write a story from the point of view of a migrating bird or a parent bird raising a cuckoo. What adventures do you have from dawn to dusk? Do you feel happy or sad?

Glossary

Antarctic Relating to the frozen area at and around the South Pole.

Arctic Relating to the frozen area at and around the North Pole.

Aviary A large enclosure for keeping birds.

Blubber The fat of penguins and sea animals.

Camouflaged Colored or patterned like the surroundings to help hide from predators.

Courtship Attracting a member of the opposite sex in order to mate.

Habitats The natural homes of plants and animals.

Hover To stay suspended in the air without moving forward.

Migration In the case of birds, moving from one region to another to escape cold winters or hot summers.

Nectar A sugary substance produced by plants to attract insects.

Parasites Animals (or plants) that live and feed on others.

Polar regions The areas around the North and the South Poles.

Predators Animals that hunt others for food.

Prey Animals that are hunted for food.

Warm-blooded Refers to animals whose body temperature stays about the same, independent of the surrounding air temperature. The skin may become hotter or colder, but the body temperature does not change.

Finding Out More

Books to Read

Birds (Eye Wonder) by Samantha Gray and Sarah Walker (DK Publishing, 2002)

Backyard Birds (Peterson Field Guides® for Young Naturalists) by Karen Stray Nolting and Jonathan Latimer (Sandpiper, 1999)

Birds (QEB Wildlife Watchers) by Terry Jennings (QEB Publishing, 2009)

Websites

National Geographic Kids
http://kids.nationalgeographic.com/kids/animals/creaturefeature/
Click on Birds to learn all about these fascinating creatures and their habitats.

National Wildlife Federation
www.nwf.org/Wildlife/Wildlife-Library.aspx
Check out this website to discover how your favorite birds live! You can also find out which birds live in your area.

Index

Page numbers in **bold** refer to photographs.

albatross **16**
animal kingdom key 5
Antarctic **13**
Arctic terns **14**

bald eagle **10**
bee-eater **14**
bills 4, 5, **7**, 8, 27
bird feeder **25**
bird of paradise 5
blackbird **21**

cage **24**, 25
cassowary **18**
chicks **21**, 22, 27
cockatoos **25**
courtship **20**
cranes **20**
cuckoo **22**

deserts 6, **15**
ducks 11, **12**, 23

eagles 8, 10
eggs 4, 11, **12**, **15**, 21, **22**, 23
emperor penguin (see penguins)
eyes 10, 26

feathers 4, **5**, **6**, **12**, **13**, 16, 21
feeding 8–11

feet 6
  clawed 6, 7, **7**, 10
  webbed 6, 7
finches 8, 11
forests 6
fulmar 11

grasslands 6

habitats 6
hawks 10
heron **15**
hoatzin 27
hummingbird **17**, 27

invertebrates 5

kingfisher **8**

lakes 6
legs **7**

mallard (see ducks)
migration 12, **13**, **14**
mountains 6

nests 11, **15**, 21, **22**, 23

ostrich **4**, 19
owls **6**, 26
oxpecker 27

parakeets **24**, 25
parrots 8, **9**
pelicans 27
penguins 13, **17**, 19, 23
peregrine falcon 10
plover 22

reed warbler **22**
rivers 6, 8, 13
roadrunner **19**

sea 6
seashores 6
secretary bird **26**
snowy owl (see owls)
stilt 7
storks 15, **23**
swallows 13
swans 11, 19, **21**
swifts 19

treecreeper **7**

vertebrates 5
vultures 6, **11**

wagtail **8**
wings 4, 16, **17**, **19**, 27
wrens 23

Picture Acknowledgements:
Bruce Coleman /J. & P. Wegner cover (inset), /Andrew Purcell 4, /Scott Nielson 6, /Mike McKavett 7(l), /Hans Reinhard 7(r), /Paolo Fioratti 8(t), /Kim Taylor 8(b), /Leonard Lee Rue 9,11, /Gordon Langsbury 14(t), /Wayne Lankinen 17(t), /C. & D. Frith 18, /Steven Kaufman 20, /Kim Taylor 21(t), /George McCarthy 22(b), /John Markham 22 (b inset), /Eckart Pott 23, 26, /Kim Taylor 25(l), /John Cancalosi 25(r) and title page (r), /Marie Read 27; FLPA /Bob Langrish 19; NHPA /Bruce Beehler 5, /Stephen Dalton 10(t) and contents page, /John Shaw 10(b) and title page, /N.R. Coulton 12, /Stephen Dalton 13(t), /B. & C. Alexander 13(b), /Alan Williams 14(b), /Vincente Canseco 15, /Bill Costner 16, /Gerard Lacz 17, /Rich Kirchner 22(t); Oxford Scientific Films © Heinz Schrempp/Okapia 24; Shutterstock, cover picture; Wayland Picture Library 21(b).